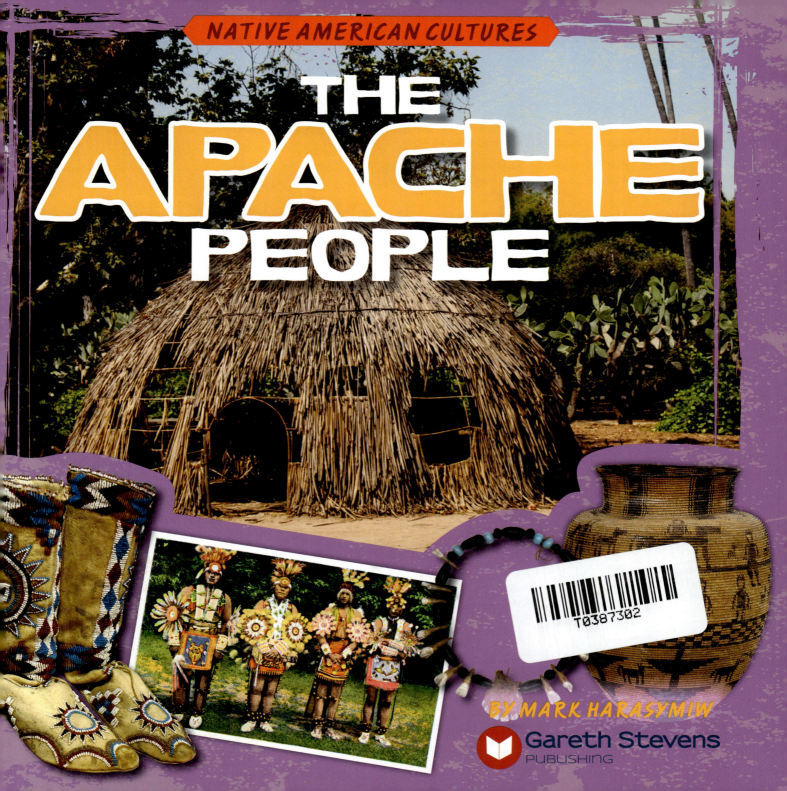

Please visit our website, www.garethstevens.com. For a free color catalog of all our high-quality books, call toll free 1-800-542-2595 or fax 1-877-542-2596.

Library of Congress Cataloging-in-Publication Data

Harasymiw, Mark.
 The Apache people / Mark Harasymiw.
     pages cm. — (Native American cultures)
 Includes index.
 ISBN 978-1-4824-1974-0 (pbk.)
 ISBN 978-1-4824-1973-3 (6 pack)
 ISBN 978-1-4824-1975-7 (library binding)
 1. Apache Indians—History—Juvenile literature. I. Title.
 E99.A6.H245 2014
 979.004'9725—dc23
 2014020529

First Edition

Published in 2015 by
Gareth Stevens Publishing
111 East 14th Street, Suite 349
New York, NY 10003

Copyright © 2015 Gareth Stevens Publishing

Designer: Sarah Liddell
Editor: Therese Shea

Photo credits: Cover, p. 1 (main) © iStockphoto.com/SWInsider; cover, p. 1 (moccasins) Daderot/Wikimedia Commons; cover, p. 1 (war dancers) Culture Club/Contributor/Hulton Archive/Getty Images; cover, p. 1 (necklace) Science & Society Picture Library/Contributor/SSPL/Getty Images; cover, p. 1 (basket) Jules Frazier/Photodisc/Getty Images; p. 5 Nativestock.com/Marilyn Angel Wynn; pp. 7, 24, 26, 29 (map) Rainer Lesniewski/Shutterstock.com; p. 8 Brian0918/Wikimedia Commons; p. 9 Travel Ink/Gallo Images/Getty Images; p. 11 photo courtesy of Curtis, Edward S./Library of Congress; p. 13 Robert Alexander/Contributor/Archive Photos/Getty Images; p. 15 SuperStock/SuperStock/Getty Images; p. 17 Apic/Contributor/Hulton Archive/Getty Images; p. 19 Martha Marks/Shutterstock.com; p. 21 MarmadukePercy/Wikimedia Commons; p. 25 LouLouPhotos/Shutterstock.com; p. 27 LAWRENCE MIGDALE/Photo Researchers/Getty Images; p. 29 Magnus Manske/Wikimedia Commons.

All rights reserved. No part of this book may be reproduced in any form without permission in writing from the publisher, except by a reviewer.

Printed in the United States of America

CPSIA compliance information: Batch #CW15GS: For further information contact Gareth Stevens, New York, New York at 1-800-542-2595.

CONTENTS

Origins of the Apache 4
The Eastern Apache 6
The Western Apache 8
Family 10
Beliefs 12
Raiding Life 14
The Americans Arrive 16
Cochise 18
Reservations 20
Regaining Control 22
San Carlos Reservation 24
White Mountain Apache Reservation . . . 26
Eastern Apache Today 28
Glossary 30
For More Information 31
Index 32

Words in the glossary appear in **bold** type the first time they are used in the text.

ORIGINS OF THE APACHE

The name "Apache" is used for several different Native American tribes. When Spanish explorers first came upon Apache in the 1500s, the tribes were living across areas that are now the southwestern United States and northern Mexico. These lands were claimed by Spain and made part of Mexico.

However, the **ancestors** of these Apache lived in western Canada and moved south around AD 1100. We know this because the Apache language is closely related to the Athabaskan language spoken by people native to western Canada.

DID YOU KNOW?

The word "Apache" comes from a Zuni Indian word meaning "enemy." The word was first used by the Spanish.

Many Apache lived in territory like this area of today's northern Mexico.

THE EASTERN APACHE

Some time before or after they moved south, the Apache separated into different tribes. The eastern Apache lived on the southern Great Plains and hunted buffalo. Each fall, they had trade fairs with the neighboring Pueblo Indians. The Apache traded buffalo meat and skins for corn and pottery.

However, this traditional way of life changed. In the early 1700s, Comanche Indians drove the Apache away from the Great Plains. Most Apache moved west into the mountains of New Mexico. However, some moved south, while others traveled east.

DID YOU KNOW?

The Apache who moved east became close **allies** to the Kiowa tribe of the Great Plains. These Apache became known as the Kiowa-Apache.

THE WESTERN APACHE

The western Apache lived in the rocky desert areas that are now Arizona and western New Mexico. There were no herds of buffalo there, so these Apache mainly ate plants that grew in desert conditions.

One of the main foods the western Apache gathered was mescal from the agave plant. They dug the bulb of the plant from the ground. The bulb can be as large as 3 feet (0.9 m) around! The Apache would cook about 1 ton (907 kg) of mescal at a time in a big pit.

WICKIUP

DID YOU KNOW?

Western Apache lived in homes called wickiups that they made from branches and leaves. Wickiups could be easily moved.

Apache ate mescal as a sweet, syrupy liquid or in dried strips.

FAMILY

The Apache lived and traveled in small groups of related families called bands. Each band chose a man as their leader. A leader could lose his position by making foolish decisions or putting the group in danger. Sometimes several bands were united under one chief.

The Apache people are matrilineal. That means their family lines are traced through the mother's side. When an Apache man got married, he lived with his wife's family. Their children belonged to the wife's **clan**. Grandparents were often the teachers of the young.

DID YOU KNOW?

While Apache men were usually the hunters, sometimes women took part in rabbit and antelope hunting.

Though it was rare for an Apache woman to become a warrior, girls learned to ride and shoot just like the boys did. Women helped defend Apache villages, too.

BELIEFS

The Apache honored a Creator spirit, from whom they asked for help and special powers. The Apache never talked about death and never called dead people by name. In fact, when a parent died, the children's names were changed so their names wouldn't remind them of their dead parent.

The Apache believed illness could be spread by seeing a body or by touching a person's things. So, when an Apache died, the body was buried quickly. Everything the dead person had owned was buried or removed.

DID YOU KNOW?

The Apache tried not to talk about owls. They believed owls contained the ghosts of the dead and brought bad luck.

Apache dancers perform the Mountain Spirit Dance in New Mexico. One reason they performed this dance was to receive help from spirits for the sick.

RAIDING LIFE

Life became tough for the Apache who had been driven away from the buffalo herds they depended on for so much. They began to look for food in other settlements.

Many hungry Apache communities became skilled at **raiding** Spanish ranches. A group of four to twelve men traveled many miles on foot. Then they'd steal as many cattle and horses as they could and race back to their homes to escape anyone who might follow. They often split up so they were even harder to track.

Apache warriors traveled light, whether on foot or on horseback. They were excellent at blending in with and hiding in their surroundings.

THE AMERICANS ARRIVE

In 1848, the United States won a war with Mexico. Much Apache land was then claimed by the United States. Soon after, large numbers of Americans began settling in Apache territory.

The Apache were forced to live on **reservations.** However, many Apache refused. Some fought to keep their lands. Others fought because reservation conditions were so tough. They were no match for the US Army, though. The last warring group of Apache, led by Geronimo, **surrendered** in 1886. Geronimo and his band were made prisoners of war and sent to Florida.

DID YOU KNOW?

With the help of a **translator,** famous Apache leader Geronimo wrote a book called *Geronimo's Story of His Life.*

Geronimo (right) stands with three of his Apache warriors in the 1880s.

COCHISE

Cochise was another well-known Apache leader. When Americans began to settle in the Southwest, Cochise tried to keep a peaceful relationship between his people, the Chiricahua Apache, and the settlers.

However, an American army officer arrested Cochise in 1861, even though the two were meeting after a **truce**. Cochise escaped—with three bullets in his body—and fought the Americans for 10 years. In 1872, he finally signed a **treaty** with the US government and lived peacefully until his death 2 years later.

Rock formations like this protected Cochise and his people after raids and when at war with the US Army.

RESERVATIONS

Life on the reservations was very hard at first. People were poor, and there were very few jobs. Bad conditions led to serious health problems, such as the spread of illness. In 1920, almost 90 percent of Jicarilla Apache children had tuberculosis, a disease that affects the lungs. The populations on all Apache reservations fell.

The US government tried to make the Apache give up their traditions. Many Apache children were forced to go to schools far away. They weren't allowed to speak the Apache language or wear traditional clothing.

DID YOU KNOW?

The Apache were one of many Native American groups forced to practice American traditions. This process was called acculturation.

These Apache children are wearing American clothing and hairstyles of the early 1900s.

21

REGAINING CONTROL

Over time, forced acculturation ended. In 1934, the US Congress passed the Indian Reorganization Act, which allowed the Apache and other native tribes to form their own governments.

In 1978, the American Indian Religious Freedom Act was passed. This meant Native Americans could go to their special places to practice their **religion**. Other American laws have made it easier for Indian tribes to operate businesses. Apache tribes have used all these laws to work to improve the lives of their people.

APACHE TIMELINE

AD 1000 — Apache move south from Canada

1500s — Spanish explorers come upon Apache in what is now the American Southwest

1700s — Comanche Indians push eastern Apache out of buffalo herd territory

1848 — United States wins territory in Southwest after war with Mexico

1870s — Apache are forced onto reservations

1872 — Cochise signs a peace treaty with the United States

1886 — Geronimo and the last of the Apache surrender to US Army

1934 — Indian Reorganization Act passed

1978 — American Indian Religious Freedom Act passed

23

SAN CARLOS RESERVATION

Most of the Apache who live in Arizona today live on reservations. The two largest in that state are the San Carlos Apache Reservation and the White Mountain Apache Reservation.

The Coolidge Dam was built on the San Carlos reservation and created a lake. The Apache sell permits to people who want to fish, hunt, hike, and camp there. The San Carlos Apache Cultural Center teaches visitors about Apache religion and traditions. The center also features and sells the work of Apache craftspeople.

About 7,000 Apache live on the San Carlos reservation today. Many are poor. There aren't many jobs on the reservation.

WHITE MOUNTAIN APACHE RESERVATION

The White Mountain Apache Reservation contains a large pine forest. Farming and raising cattle are important industries there. Apache on this land also run a winter and summer resort. The mountains, lakes, and streams draw people who want to ski, fish, and canoe. There's also a large **casino** that attracts many visitors.

The White Mountain Apache Cultural Center displays historic objects and modern Apache arts and crafts. A re-creation of an Apache village is located nearby.

The White Mountain Apache Tribal Fair and **Rodeo** occurs every September on the White Mountain Apache Reservation.

EASTERN APACHE TODAY

The eastern Apache live on different reservations today. The Mescalero Apache of southern New Mexico raise cattle, sell timber, and run a resort. In northern New Mexico, the Jicarilla Apache earn money from oil on their land. Other Apache reservations have founded businesses to help their people as well.

There are tens of thousands of Apache today in the United States. Most live in modern houses and dress in modern clothes. However, the Apache still have to fight to keep their land. They also work hard to continue their traditions in our changing world.

DID YOU KNOW?

Today, there are more than 2,000 oil and gas wells on Jicarilla Apache land!

SKI APACHE, MESCALERO APACHE RESERVATION

Two other populations of eastern Apache are located in Oklahoma: the Apache Tribe of Oklahoma and the Fort Sill Apache.

GLOSSARY

ally: one of two or more people or groups who work together

ancestor: a relative who lived long before someone

casino: a place where people gamble, or play games of chance and risk

clan: a group of related families

raid: to suddenly attack

religion: a belief in and way of honoring a god or gods

reservation: land set aside by the US government for Native Americans

rodeo: a contest of many events involving cowboy skills

surrender: to give up

translator: one who tells what words in one language mean in another

treaty: an agreement between groups

truce: an agreement to end fighting for a period of time

FOR MORE INFORMATION

BOOKS

Behnke, Alison. *The Apaches*. Minneapolis, MN: Lerner Publications, 2006.

Kissock, Heather, and Jordan McGill. *Apache*. New York: NY: Weigl Publishers, 2010.

Sullivan, George. *Geronimo: Apache Renegade*. New York, NY: Sterling, 2010.

WEBSITES

Apache Indian Fact Sheet
www.bigorrin.org/apache_kids.htm
Do you have a question about the Apache? Find the answer here.

Purple Hawk's Nest
impurplehawk.com/index.html
Check out this award-winning website including Apache music, photos, and facts about Apache life.

Publisher's note to educators and parents: Our editors have carefully reviewed these websites to ensure that they are suitable for students. Many websites change frequently, however, and we cannot guarantee that a site's future contents will continue to meet our high standards of quality and educational value. Be advised that students should be closely supervised whenever they access the Internet.

INDEX

acculturation 20, 22

American Indian Religious Freedom Act 22, 23

Americans 16, 18

Arizona 8, 24

bands 10, 16

buffalo 6, 8, 14, 23

Canada 4, 23

Chiricahua Apache 18

clan 10

Cochise 18, 19, 23

Creator spirit 12

eastern Apache 6, 23, 28, 29

Geronimo 16, 17, 23

Great Plains 6

Indian Reorganization Act 22, 23

Jicarilla Apache 20, 28

Kiowa-Apache 6

language 4, 20

mescal 8, 9

Mescalero Apache 28

Mexico 4, 5, 16, 23

Mountain Spirit Dance 13

New Mexico 6, 8, 13, 28

raiding 14, 19

reservations 16, 20, 23, 24, 25, 28

San Carlos Apache Reservation 24, 25

Southwest 18, 23

Spanish 4, 14, 23

United States 4, 16, 23, 28

western Apache 8

White Mountain Apache Reservation 24, 26, 27

wickiups 8

NATIVE AMERICAN CULTURES

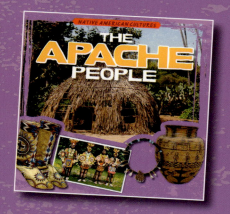
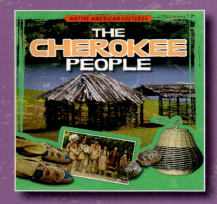
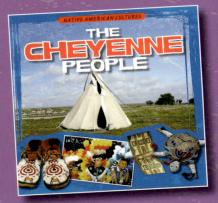
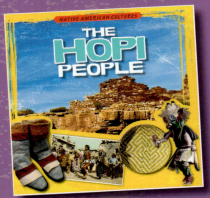

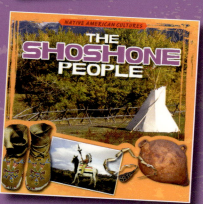

Levels: GR: N; DRA: 30

ISBN: 978-1-4824-1974-0
6-pack ISBN: 978-1-4824-1973-3

Gareth Stevens
PUBLISHING